BL 3.7
pts 0.5

Q

THE SEARCH FOR THE
BOOK OF THOTH

A RETELLING BY CARI MEISTER　　ILLUSTRATED BY JARED OSTERHOLD

PICTURE WINDOW BOOKS
a capstone imprint

CAST OF CHARACTERS

Thoth (THOTH): god of wisdom

Neferkaptah (neh-fehr-CAP-tah): Egyptian prince; husband of Ahura; father to Merab

Ahura (eh-HUR-ah): wife of Neferkaptah; mother to Merab

Merab (MEHR-uhb): son of Neferkaptah and Ahura

 # WORDS TO KNOW

barge—a large, flat ship

embalm—to preserve a dead body from decay

ibis—a tropical bird with a downwardly curving bill

ka—the spiritual essence of a dead person

myth—a story told by people in ancient times; myths often tried to explain natural events

pharaoh—a king of ancient Egypt

scroll—a roll of papyrus, leather, or parchment that has ancient writings on it

sycamore—a kind of wood

tomb—a room or building that holds a dead body

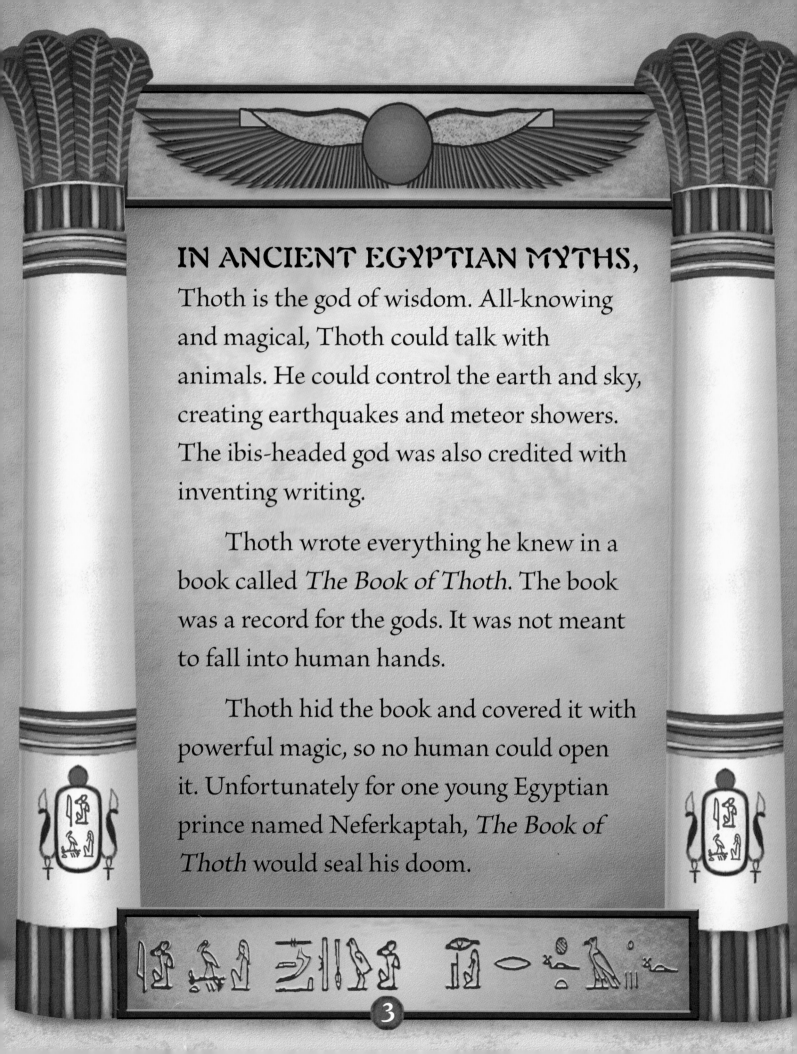

IN ANCIENT EGYPTIAN MYTHS, Thoth is the god of wisdom. All-knowing and magical, Thoth could talk with animals. He could control the earth and sky, creating earthquakes and meteor showers. The ibis-headed god was also credited with inventing writing.

Thoth wrote everything he knew in a book called *The Book of Thoth*. The book was a record for the gods. It was not meant to fall into human hands.

Thoth hid the book and covered it with powerful magic, so no human could open it. Unfortunately for one young Egyptian prince named Neferkaptah, *The Book of Thoth* would seal his doom.

Prince Neferkaptah examined the ancient scrolls for the hundredth time.

"There must be something I have not studied!" he said.

But as the day wore on, he couldn't find anything new to add to his knowledge.

"How can I become the greatest magician of all time, if there is nothing more for me to study?" he sighed.

Neferkaptah's young son ran into the study, followed by Ahura, his wife.

"Merab! Come, sit on my lap. I will teach you a spell," said Neferkaptah.

Ahura laughed. "He's too young for that!" she said. "Come outside and eat. You've been in here all day—the sun has almost set!"

Although Neferkaptah liked to study, he always made time for his family, whom he loved dearly.

After finishing dinner, the prince kissed Merab on the head. "I must get back to work," he said.

"Perhaps you should go to the temple and pray to the gods," said Ahura.

"You're right," he said. "It's been too long since I visited the temple. I will go now. Then I will get back to my studies."

As Neferkaptah sped up the temple steps, a carving on the wall caught his eye.

An old priest stood in the doorway and laughed. "You will find no new knowledge in that carving!" he said. "You've studied it many times. But listen carefully! I can tell you how you can gain the knowledge of the gods!"

"What do you mean?" asked Neferkaptah.

"Thoth, the god of wisdom, wrote down all of his secrets in a book called *The Book of Thoth*," said the priest.

Neferkaptah nodded. "I've heard of it," he said, "but Thoth hid it. No one knows where it is."

The priest smiled. "I know where it is!" he said. "Give me 100 silver bars, and promise to bury me like a king when I die. Then I will tell you!"

Neferkaptah agreed at once.

9

Neferkaptah ran home and prepared the royal barge. "I want to sail at once!" he said to Ahura. "You and Merab must come with me. I know where to find *The Book of Thoth*."

Ahura was hesitant. "The book of the gods?" she asked. "I don't think we should touch it. It might bring trouble."

But Neferkaptah was thinking only about finding *The Book of Thoth*. He did not even seem to hear his wife's warning.

The family left their home in Memphis, Egypt and sailed up the Nile River until they came to the town of Koptos.

When the local temple priests saw the royal barge approach, they came down to the water's edge.

"Welcome!" they said. "What has brought you to Koptos?"

"We've come for *The Book of Thoth*," said Neferkaptah.

The priests were surprised. Very few Egyptians knew about the book's location.

13

14.

"It's here," said a priest. "It's underwater, in an iron box. In the iron box is a bronze box; in the bronze box, there is a sycamore box; in the sycamore box, there is an ivory and ebony box; in the ivory and ebony box, there is a silver box; in the silver box, there is a golden box. And inside the golden box is *The Book of Thoth*.

"But be warned, young prince! The book cannot be touched by human hands! The gods have surrounded it with magic. A serpent that cannot be slain guards it. Come feast with us, then take your barge home. If you try to touch the book, you will seal your doom."

The priest's words scared Ahura. But the prince just smiled. "Do you think I've come all this way unprepared?" he said.

"I know of the book's dangers. They do not scare me. I'm a prince, and the finest magician around. Surely I can defeat the spells that surround this ancient book. After we feast, you will see!"

When the royal family and priests were done feasting, Neferkaptah stood up.

"I cannot delay. Ahura, Merab—you stay here while I get the book. Soon I will know everything the gods do!"

Again, Ahura tried to stop her husband, but it was no use.

Neferkaptah ran down to the river. He picked up some mud in his hands, molded it, and uttered a spell. The mud was magically transformed into a group of strong men.

Neferkaptah breathed life into the men and commanded them, "Work for me! Go to the river's bottom and find *The Book of Thoth*!"

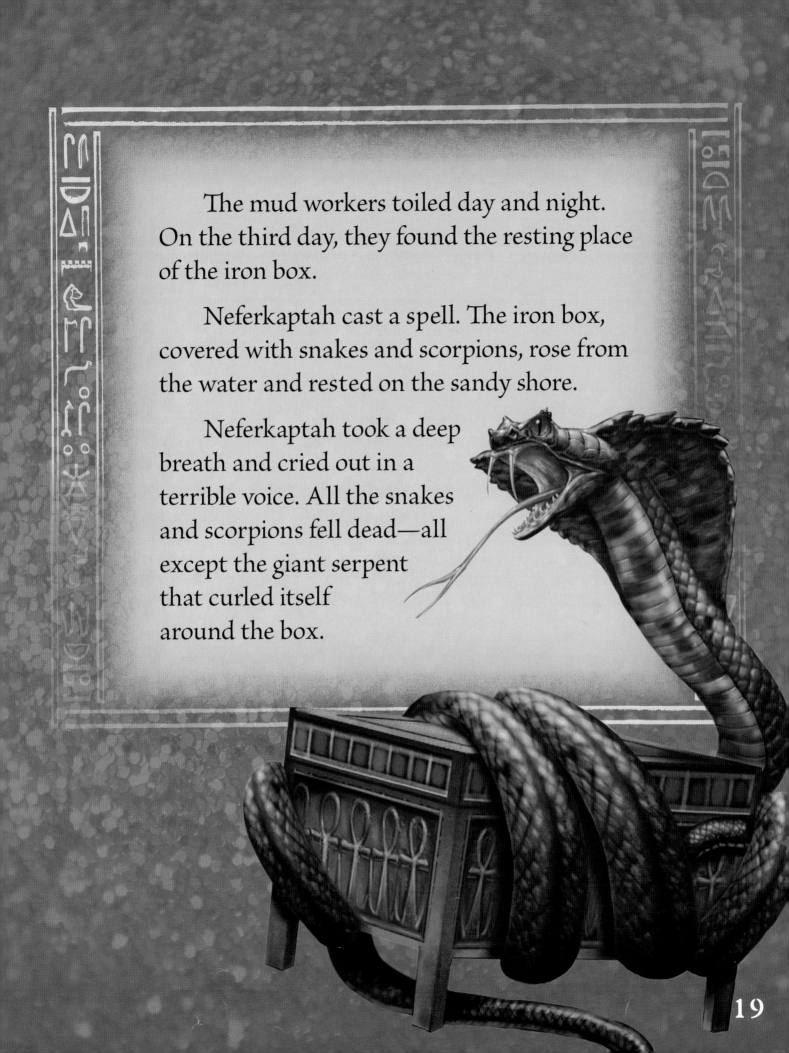

The mud workers toiled day and night. On the third day, they found the resting place of the iron box.

Neferkaptah cast a spell. The iron box, covered with snakes and scorpions, rose from the water and rested on the sandy shore.

Neferkaptah took a deep breath and cried out in a terrible voice. All the snakes and scorpions fell dead—all except the giant serpent that curled itself around the box.

Neferkaptah cast spell after spell, but nothing worked on the magical serpent.

He pulled the sword from his belt and cut off the creature's head. But to his horror, the serpent's head reattached itself!

Ahura, who was watching from the temple, screamed.

Neferkaptah sliced the beast again. This time, he threw the head into the river. Again, the serpent's head magically reattached itself.

The prince was growing tired. He had to think quickly. "I know!" he said as he sliced off the snake's head for the third time.

Before the snake's head could reattach itself, Neferkaptah threw sand onto the serpent's open wound. When the head tried to reattach, the sand blocked the magic.

The snake couldn't move, but it wasn't dead. Its eyes watched Neferkaptah walk over to the iron box.

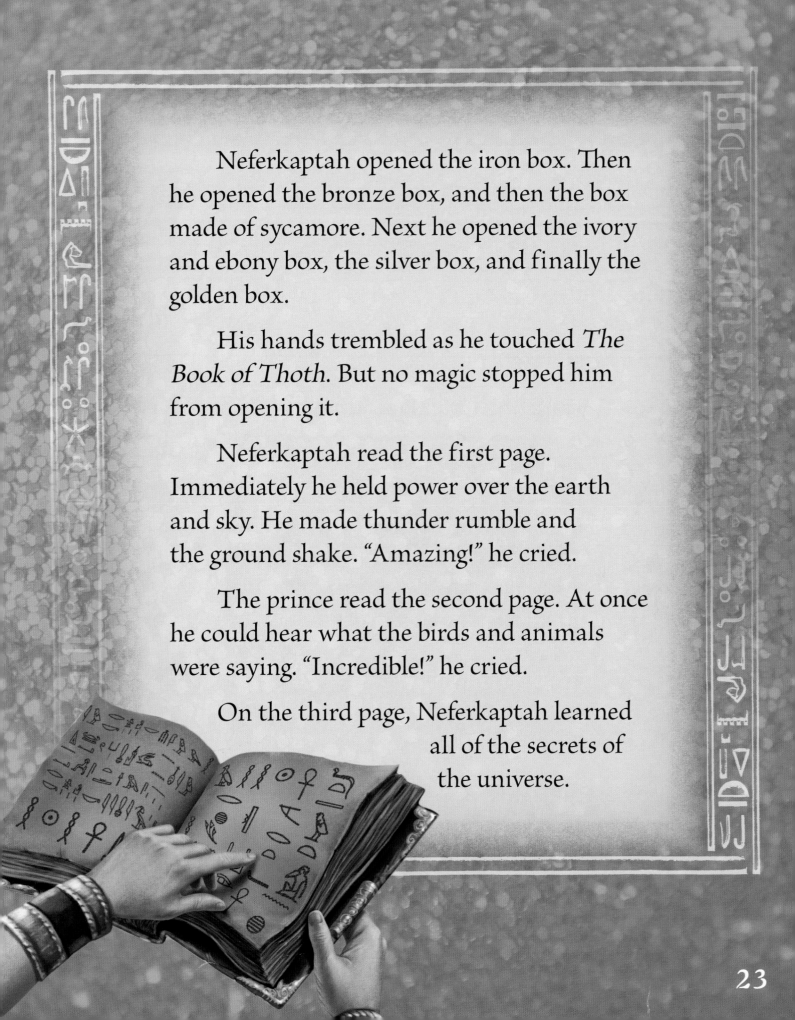

Neferkaptah opened the iron box. Then he opened the bronze box, and then the box made of sycamore. Next he opened the ivory and ebony box, the silver box, and finally the golden box.

His hands trembled as he touched *The Book of Thoth*. But no magic stopped him from opening it.

Neferkaptah read the first page. Immediately he held power over the earth and sky. He made thunder rumble and the ground shake. "Amazing!" he cried.

The prince read the second page. At once he could hear what the birds and animals were saying. "Incredible!" he cried.

On the third page, Neferkaptah learned all of the secrets of the universe.

Neferkaptah couldn't wait to share the secrets with Ahura.

"Come, Ahura!" he called. "Read these pages! You too shall know the powers of the gods!"

After reading the pages, Ahura also gained power over the earth and sky. She knew the language of the animals, and learned all the universe's secrets.

Soon the family boarded the barge for home. They had hardly started to move when a terrible power seized Merab.

"What's happening?" screamed Ahura as Merab was thrown into the water.

Neferkaptah quickly spoke a powerful spell. Merab's body returned to the ship, but he was already dead.

"My son!" cried Neferkaptah. "What happened to you?"

Although Merab was dead, his spirit, called a ka, spoke. "Thoth knows you found his book of magic," said his ka. "It was Thoth's power that threw me into the river and drowned me. He wants to punish you!"

A moment later, the same power took hold of Ahura. She was thrown into the river.

Neferkaptah cried and tore his clothes. He yelled out more spells. Ahura's body returned to the barge, but it was too late. She was dead.

Neferkaptah soon embalmed his wife and son, and buried them in a tomb in Koptos. "I must go tell my father of my misfortune," he said.

He boarded the royal barge and once more set out for home. However, when the barge arrived in Memphis, the prince did not step off of it.

Neferkaptah's father, a pharaoh, found his son lying on the floor of the barge, dead. *The Book of Thoth* had been tied around Neferkaptah's body. The pharaoh cried out, "Let this be a lesson to all! Do not seek the knowledge that belongs to the gods!"

With a heavy heart, the pharaoh placed Neferkaptah and *The Book of Thoth* in a tomb. He sealed the tomb, so no one would ever share Neferkaptah's disastrous fate.

READ MORE

Adamson, Heather. *Ancient Egypt: An Interactive History Adventure.* You Choose Books. Mankato, Minn.: Capstone Press, 2010.

Elgin, Kathy. *Egyptian Myths.* Myths from Many Lands. New York: Skivvy Books, 2009.

Williams, Marcia. *Ancient Egypt: Tales of Gods and Pharaohs.* Somerville, Mass.: Candlewick Press, 2011.

INTERNET SITES

FactHound offers a safe, fun way to find Internet sites related to this book. All of the sites on FactHound have been researched by our staff.

Here's all you do:

Visit *www.facthound.com*

Type in this code: 9781404871519

Check out projects, games and lots more at
www.capstonekids.com

LOOK FOR ALL THE BOOKS IN THE EGYPTIAN MYTHS SERIES:

Thanks to our adviser for his expertise and advice:
Terry Flaherty, PhD
Professor of English
Minnesota State University, Mankato

Editor: Shelly Lyons
Designer: Ted Williams
Art Director: Nathan Gassman
Production Specialist: Danielle Ceminsky
The illustrations in this book were created with watercolors, gouache, acrylics, and digitally.
Artistic Effects
Shutterstock: Goran Bogicevic, Kristina Divinchuk, Shvaygert Ekaterina, Vladislav Gurfinkel

Picture Window Books
1710 Roe Crest Drive
North Mankato, MN 56003
www.capstonepub.com

All books published by Picture Window Books are manufactured with paper containing at least 10 percent post-consumer waste.

Library of Congress Cataloging-in-Publication Data
Meister, Cari.
The search for the book of Thoth : a retelling / by Cari Meister; illustrated by Jared Osterhold.
    p. cm. — (Egyptian myths)
 Includes index.
 "A Capstone imprint."
ISBN 978-1-4048-7151-9 (library binding)
ISBN 978-1-4048-7243-1 (paperback)
 1. Gods, Egyptian—Juvenile literature. 2. Goddesses, Egyptian—Juvenile literature. 3. Mythology, Egyptian—Juvenile literature. I. Osterhold, Jared. II. Title. III. Series: Egyptian myths.
 BL2450.G6M47 2012
 299.3113—dc23
                                            2011025861

Printed in the United States of America in Stevens Point, Wisconsin.
102011   006404WZS12